# Countercyclical Capital Regime Revisited: Tests of Robustness*

# Countercyclical Capital Regime Revisited:
## Tests of Robustness

## Abstract

This paper tests the robustness of key elements of the Smith and Weiher (2012) countercyclical capital regime. Such tests are now possible given that the recent house price cycle is nearing its end. The recent house price cycle allows for rigorous out-of-sample testing because it encompassed state-level house price cycles of significantly greater magnitude than those observable by Smith and Weiher during the design period of their stress test. The tests of robustness presented herein support the conclusion that the Smith and Weiher countercyclical capital regime should produce capital requirements sufficient to ensure an entity would remain solvent during severe house price cycles. This conclusion is strongly supported by a back-test of the countercyclical framework using Fannie Mae's historical book of business. If the countercyclical capital requirement had been in place during the run-up to the recent house price bubble, Fannie Mae would have been sufficiently capitalized to withstand losses it sustained in the subsequent housing crisis. This result is particularly noteworthy given that key components of the Smith and Weiher stress test were designed based upon pre-2002 data. Individual examinations of the trend line, trough, and time path components of the Smith and Weiher countercyclical capital regime all indicate that the underlying methodology is stable and robust. We also find that the countercyclical-related patterns in capital requirements will not vary when the stress test is applied to different credit models, but the level of capital required may vary appreciably. This suggests that over-reliance on any one credit model may not be prudent.

# Countercyclical Capital Regime Revisited:
## Tests of Robustness

## Executive Summary

Smith and Weiher (2012) introduce a countercyclical capital methodology. This paper tests the robustness of key aspects of that methodology. Such tests are now possible because the recent house price cycle is nearly completed. The recent cycle allows for rigorous out-of-sample testing because it encompassed much larger state-level house price cycles than those observable by Smith and Weiher during the design period of their stress test.[1]

The Smith and Weiher countercyclical methodology is best described as a dynamically determined stress test for mortgage assets. It is countercyclical in that the resulting capital requirements are increasing during the upswing of a house price bubble and decreasing as house prices fall. If these capital requirements were broadly applied, both outcomes would serve to mitigate the amplitude of a house price cycle. The severity of the Smith and Weiher countercyclical stress test, as measured by the down shock of a house price index (HPI), is entirely a function of the current level of HPI and a pre-determined trough, expressed as a percentage of the long-run trend in HPI. Thus, the severity of the stress test is not fixed, but instead changes over time corresponding to deviations of HPI from its long-run trend. As a result, the Smith and Weiher approach departs from traditional historically-based stress tests in that its severity, or extent of the HPI decline (shock), is not constrained or bounded to what has been observed historically. By design, if HPI were to rise higher above long-run trend than historically observed, the applicable countercyclical HPI shock and resulting capital requirements would increase correspondingly. This dynamic design makes the Smith and Weiher regime countercyclical in nature.

The Smith and Weiher stress test is also rules-based and does not depend on the subjective views of any analyst or regulator. This deterministic feature facilitates back-testing of the countercyclical stress test to assess how resulting capital requirements might have evolved during past cycles. Such back-testing is imperative in order to assess whether the stress test will produce sufficient capital requirements under severe house price cycles.

---

[1] The causes of the housing cycle are outside the scope of this paper and the authors make no assertions about the cause of this cycle.

The first set of robustness tests finds that the countercyclical-related patterns in capital requirements will not vary when the countercyclical stress test is applied to different credit models, but the level of capital required may vary appreciably. This suggests that over-reliance on any one credit model may not be prudent for an entity or regulator. It also shows that the countercyclical stress test is stable across credit models in that the expected patterns for countercyclical capital requirements appear for all credit models both across origination year and across time for a given origination year cohort of loans.

Next we assess how well the countercyclical capital regime would have worked had it been in place for Fannie Mae during the critical year of 2008. We find that even for the least conservative credit model, the countercyclical stress test produced capital requirements that were more than sufficient to have covered the substantial losses suffered by Fannie Mae during the recent housing crisis. This is a particularly powerful result because the key components of the stress test were based on pre-2002 data. This leads us to conclude that, because of its dynamic structure, the Smith and Weiher countercyclical capital regime should produce capital requirements sufficient to ensure an entity would remain solvent during severe house price cycles.

We also tested how consistent the capital requirements would be if the data used to establish the key parameters of the stress test were updated to incorporate the now nearly completed and very severe house price cycle. In addition, we analyzed how well the original Smith and Weiher trend, trough, and time-path estimates compared when evaluated against the actual experience of the recent house price cycle. We find that Smith and Weiher predictions of the trend line, trough, and time path components compare very well to or are more conservative than the actual data of the recent cycle, data which was not considered in the original calibration of those components. This is still further support for the conclusion that design for each of the key elements of the countercyclical stress test is both stable and robust across stress environments, including those yet to occur.

# Countercyclical Capital Regime Revisited: Tests of Robustness

## Introduction

Smith and Weiher (2012) introduce a countercyclical capital regime that embodies a stress test designed for mortgage-related assets. This paper tests the robustness of key elements of that methodology. Such tests are now possible given that the recent house price cycle is nearing its end. The recent house price cycle allows for rigorous out-of-sample testing because it encompassed state-level house price cycles of significantly greater magnitude than those observable by Smith and Weiher during the design period of their stress test.

In this paper, we expand on Smith and Weiher by presenting a number of tests of robustness regarding their methodology. Specifically, we examine each of the key design elements of the stress test, including construction of the trend line, the trough, and the time-path. We also expand on the empirical results presented by Smith and Weiher by showing how the resulting capital requirements might vary when their countercyclical stress test is applied using several different credit models. Further, we back-test to evaluate how well the countercyclical capital regime would have performed had it been in place for Fannie Mae in 2008, likely the peak moment in terms of required capital during the recent housing price cycle.

## Background

Dynamically Determined Design: The Smith and Weiher countercyclical capital methodology is best described as a dynamically determined stress test for mortgage assets. Specifically, the severity of the stress test, as measured by the down shock of a house price index (HPI), is entirely a function of the current level of HPI and a pre-determined trough, expressed as a percentage of the long-run trend in HPI. As a result, the severity of the stress test is not fixed, but instead changes over time corresponding to deviations of HPI from its long-run trend. When HPI rises (falls) with respect to trend, the magnitude of the shock increases (decreases). Consequently, the stress test severity increases during the upswing of a house price bubble, and decreases as house prices fall. Furthermore and most importantly, the Smith and Weiher approach departs from traditional historically-based stress tests in that its severity, or extent of the HPI decline (shock), is not constrained or bounded to what has been observed historically. By design, if HPI were to rise higher above long-run trend than historically observed, the applicable countercyclical HPI shock would increase correspondingly. This dynamic design makes the Smith and Weiher regime countercyclical in nature.

In the Smith and Weiher framework, the extent that HPI can fall below trend is predetermined which allows the HPI shock associated with any current, past, or future level of HPI to be calculated directly and with ease. Thus, even though the HPI shock is dynamic rather than fixed, it is rules-based and not dependent on the subjective views of any analyst or regulator. This deterministic feature also facilitates back-testing of the countercyclical stress test to assess how resulting capital requirements might have evolved during past cycles. Such back-testing is imperative in order to have a perspective on whether the stress test is of sufficient severity given the credit model being used. Further, this design feature would permit an entity or regulator to engage in future capital planning under any forecast of future HPI with the confidence that the estimated capital requirements will closely approximate the actual capital requirements should that forecast of HPI be realized.

Finally, since the worst-case trough (or depth to which HPI will fall) is preset and only updated when a new HPI cycle has been completed (and may not change even then), the structure of the stress test is such that the resulting capital requirement for a pool or vintage of loans should be highest on the date of acquisition, and then proceed to decline with time as the loans age.[2] Under the Smith and Weiher framework, the HPI shock is structured to be as severe on day one of acquisition as could reasonably be expected to occur. This means that the resulting capital required at acquisition should represent the full capitalization of that pool of loans, or the most capital ever to be needed for the life of those loans. Such up front knowledge of maximum required capital affords the acquiring entity a level of certainty with regard to capital requirements and capital management that does not exist with pro-cyclical capital regimes, which is a major reason why pro-cyclical capital regimes fail (see also – Frame et al., 2013).

---

[2]Our empirical results reveal that, under extreme stress, full capitalization at acquisition may not be strictly achieved for a given origination year (cohort) of loans. We discuss this issue in greater detail below.

## Overview of Robustness Tests

A well designed stress test must first and foremost result in capital requirements specific to an entity that are sufficient to ensure that the entity remains solvent during periods of significant financial stress. In order to make such an assessment of the Smith and Weiher countercyclical capital regime, however, we must ensure that any evaluation will not be dependent on the particular credit model employed. In other words, we seek to verify that the countercyclical capital methodology will produce relatively stable and consistent capital requirements when applied using different credit models. Building on the results across credit models, we then assess how well the countercyclical capital regime would have worked had it been in place for Fannie Mae during the critical year of 2008.

The remainder of the paper examines the robustness of several facets of the Smith and Weiher methodology. Specifically, we evaluate how consistent the capital requirements are likely to be if the data used to establish several of the key parameters of the stress test were updated to incorporate the now nearly completed recent and very severe house price cycle. We note that Smith and Weiher, working in 2010, chose to estimate trend, trough, and time path (at the state level) using only pre-2002 data, so as not to include the current and incomplete house price cycle. Now that the recent house price cycle is very nearly complete, we are able to present analyses on how well the original Smith and Weiher trend, trough, and time-path estimates performed when evaluated against an actual experience that was more severe than any historical experience included in the data set used to both develop and calibrate the original stress test design.

### Countercyclical Capital Requirements Compared Across Credit Models

In analyzing their empirical results, Smith and Weiher focus on whether the patterns of capital requirements that result from the application of the countercyclical stress test are consistent with the goal of a countercyclical capital regime both for new originations over the cycle and for a given origination-year cohort of loans over time. Below, we extend that analysis to the results from three other credit models.

Smith and Weiher used their countercyclical stress test to estimate capital requirements applicable to Fannie Mae's book of fixed-rate 30-year loans as of September 30, 2003, 2005, 2006, 2007, 2008 and 2010. They modeled credit losses

using an internally developed credit model (Model V1).  Their results, reproduced
in Table 1, represent the discounted present value of estimated life-time credit
losses under countercyclical stress as a percent of outstanding unpaid principal
balances (UPB) at each September 30th date.  For each simulation start year
shown, Smith and Weiher used a representative sample of 2-million loans.

### Table 1
#### FHFA Default and Prepayment Model V1

| Capital Charges as Percent of UPB (UPB at start of simulation) | Simulation Start Year (as of September 30th) | | | | | |
|---|---|---|---|---|---|---|
| Origination Year | 2003 | 2005 | 2006 | 2007 | 2008 | 2010 |
| 2001 | 1.45% | 1.19% | 1.11% | 1.02% | 0.80% | 1.35% |
| 2002 | 3.34% | 2.11% | 2.06% | 1.78% | 1.34% | 2.52% |
| 2003 | 3.51% | 1.94% | 1.80% | 1.49% | 1.12% | 1.91% |
| 2004 | | 5.11% | 4.92% | 4.23% | 3.34% | 5.32% |
| 2005 | | 9.97% | 9.83% | 8.78% | 7.54% | 11.19% |
| 2006 | | | 15.84% | 14.69% | 13.51% | 20.82% |
| 2007 | | | | 16.88% | 14.68% | 22.11% |
| 2008 | | | | | 8.79% | 12.27% |
| 2009 | | | | | | 2.19% |
| 2010 | | | | | | 2.62% |
| Total | 2.95% | 4.21% | 6.80% | 8.93% | 8.24% | 8.21% |

In keeping with their expectations on how the countercyclical capital regime
should work, the results in Table 1 (down the diagonal) show that the
countercyclical capital requirement for newly-originated loans increases when
house prices rise during credit expansions (2003-2007) and then declines when
house prices fall in credit contractions (2007-2010).  Furthermore, as house prices
heated up in 2003, capital requirements not only grew, but grew rapidly – from
3.51 percent in 2003 to 9.97 percent two years later to 15.84 percent and 16.88
percent in the following two years.  Again, in keeping with an intended result,
both the level and rate of growth of required capital likely would not have been
accommodated by Fannie Mae.  More likely, Fannie Mae would have been
incented to reduce the volume of loans they acquired and guaranteed and also to
tighten underwriting standards.

The other key pattern to observe in the results is whether the capital
requirement for a given cohort of loans is largest in the year of acquisition,

consistent with the goal of full capitalization up front. In support of this design goal, countercyclical capital, expressed as a fraction of the outstanding balances of loans in each origination-year cohort (each horizontal line), declines for all origination-year cohorts in each year subsequent to the year of acquisition, except in 2010.[3]

In 2010, the countercyclical capital ratio increased for each origination-year cohort over the percentage that would have been required for that same origination-year cohort in 2008 and was in several cases a larger percentage than would have been required in the year of origination. This is due to the fact that mortgage rates were falling encouraging rapid prepayments, while at the same time a large volume of loans were subjected to extended foreclosure timelines (see also – Cordell et al., 2013). As a result, troubled loans increased dramatically as a percentage of the outstanding balance of every cohort. Nonetheless, as shown below for Model V1, the capital requirement in actual dollars would have fallen or stayed about the same, never exceeding the capital requirement on the day of acquisition.

We extend the Smith and Weiher analysis by applying their countercyclical stress test using three additional credit models, including an updated version of the internal credit model initially used by Smith and Weiher (Model V2).[4] The other two credit models used include those available from Lender Processing Services – Applied Analytics, Black Knight (formerly Lender Processing Services Applied Analytics, LPS-AA) and Andrew Davidson and Company (ADCO Loan Dynamics Model or LDM).

Tables 2 through 4 show the countercyclical capital requirements that result from applying the Smith and Weiher stress test using each of the three additional credit models. Note that, to lessen our computational burden, we only test portfolios as of September 30, 2005, 2007 and 2010 in applying the countercyclical stress test to the ADCO LDM and Black Knight models.[5]

---

[3] It is likely the 2009 results would appear very similar to those in 2010, but Smith and Weiher did not examine that year to verify.

[4] Models V1 and V2 use as their dependent variable the first time a loan becomes 90-days delinquent. This is not a terminal state, as is voluntary or involuntary prepayment or maturity. As a result, Model V1 uses a bridge to a publicly available loss severity model under the assumption that a historically-generated fraction of loans that are 90-days delinquent resolve with a loss. Model V2 includes a bridge predicated on better and more complete data, including alternative foreclosure resolutions as well as foreclosures. It also includes a new proprietary loss severity model.

[5] For comparative analysis, the same two million samples of Fannie Mae 30-year fixed rate loans employed by Smith and Weiher were used in all of the alternative credit model analyses.

# Table 2
FHFA Default and Prepayment Model V2

| Capital Charges as Percent of UPB (UPB at start of simulation) | Simulation Start Year (as of September 30th) | | | | | |
|---|---|---|---|---|---|---|
| Origination Year | 2003 | 2005 | 2006 | 2007 | 2008 | 2010 |
| 2001 | 1.04% | 0.94% | 0.87% | 0.79% | 0.65% | 1.15% |
| 2002 | 2.14% | 1.39% | 1.34% | 1.17% | 0.93% | 1.72% |
| 2003 | 2.16% | 1.14% | 1.02% | 0.87% | 0.69% | 1.19% |
| 2004 | | 2.95% | 2.65% | 2.27% | 1.88% | 3.26% |
| 2005 | | 5.64% | 5.12% | 4.47% | 3.98% | 6.69% |
| 2006 | | | 8.43% | 7.96% | 7.68% | 13.90% |
| 2007 | | | | 9.02% | 8.33% | 14.85% |
| 2008 | | | | | 3.86% | 6.39% |
| 2009 | | | | | | 0.61% |
| 2010 | | | | | | 0.69% |
| Total | 1.87% | 2.46% | 3.66% | 4.80% | 4.46% | 4.79% |

# Table 3
Black Knight Credit Model

| Capital Charges as Percent of UPB (UPB at start of simulation) | Simulation Start Year (as of September 30th) | | | | | |
|---|---|---|---|---|---|---|
| Origination Year | 2003 | 2005 | 2006 | 2007 | 2008 | 2010 |
| 2001 | | 1.06% | | 0.96% | | 2.24% |
| 2002 | | 1.90% | | 1.64% | | 3.13% |
| 2003 | | 1.46% | | 1.24% | | 1.99% |
| 2004 | | 3.59% | | 3.09% | | 4.77% |
| 2005 | | 6.08% | | 5.74% | | 7.82% |
| 2006 | | | | 10.11% | | 14.55% |
| 2007 | | | | 10.49% | | 14.44% |
| 2008 | | | | | | 6.44% |
| 2009 | | | | | | 0.66% |
| 2010 | | | | | | 0.83% |
| Total | | 2.86% | | 5.95% | | 5.46% |

Table 4

**ADCO LDM Credit Model**

| Capital Charges as Percent of UPB (UPB at start of simulation) | Simulation Start Year (as of September 30th) | | | | | |
|---|---|---|---|---|---|---|
| Origination Year | 2003 | 2005 | 2006 | 2007 | 2008 | 2010 |
| 2001 | | 2.06% | | 1.71% | | 1.81% |
| 2002 | | 2.59% | | 1.95% | | 2.01% |
| 2003 | | 2.27% | | 1.57% | | 1.38% |
| 2004 | | 5.43% | | 3.92% | | 3.23% |
| 2005 | | 9.57% | | 8.05% | | 6.64% |
| 2006 | | | | 13.26% | | 12.83% |
| 2007 | | | | 14.46% | | 13.59% |
| 2008 | | | | | | 5.82% |
| 2009 | | | | | | 0.90% |
| 2010 | | | | | | 1.13% |
| Total | | 4.45% | | 8.02% | | 4.93% |

Patterns and Full Capitalization at Acquisition: A review of the results in Tables 1-4 shows that the same patterns emerge regardless of the credit model. We can conclude, therefore, that the Smith and Weiher countercyclical design should produce consistent results across alternative credit models. Specifically, the primary pattern that should result from their design is evident across models, where capital requirements for new originations increase (decrease) as housing prices are rising (falling) relative to long-term trend.

We also find that the 2010 exception, an increase in the percentage capital requirement, appears in each of the four models. In order to examine whether Smith and Weiher's second outcome related design goal is achieved, that the capital requirements are in fact largest in the year of acquisition, we converted the percentage requirements to dollar amounts by simply multiplying the percentages by outstanding balances. We then normalized these dollar amounts by dividing by origination year countercyclical losses. Tables 5-8 show the results, where the capital requirements in absolute (dollar) terms are standardized at 100 in the year of acquisition.

## Table 5

| Capital Charges in Dollars Normalized to 100 (New Originations) | Simulation Start Year (as of September 30th) | | | | | |
|---|---|---|---|---|---|---|
| Origination Year | 2003 | 2005 | 2006 | 2007 | 2008 | 2010 |
| 2001 | | | | | | |
| 2002 | | | | | | |
| 2003 | 100 | 45 | 33 | 21 | 13 | 16 |
| 2004 | | | | | | |
| 2005 | | 100 | 110 | 76 | 54 | 57 |
| 2006 | | | 100 | 95 | 67 | 60 |
| 2007 | | | | 100 | 90 | 77 |
| 2008 | | | | | 100 | 94 |
| 2009 | | | | | | |
| 2010 | | | | | | 100 |

FHFA Default and Prepayment Model V1, Normalized

## Table 6

| Capital Charges in Dollars Normalized to 100 (New Originations) | Simulation Start Year (as of September 30th) | | | | | |
|---|---|---|---|---|---|---|
| Origination Year | 2003 | 2005 | 2006 | 2007 | 2008 | 2010 |
| 2001 | | | | | | |
| 2002 | | | | | | |
| 2003 | 100 | 43 | 30 | 20 | 13 | 16 |
| 2004 | | | | | | |
| 2005 | | 100 | 101 | 68 | 50 | 59 |
| 2006 | | | 100 | 96 | 71 | 73 |
| 2007 | | | | 100 | 95 | 94 |
| 2008 | | | | | 100 | 110 |
| 2009 | | | | | | |
| 2010 | | | | | | 100 |

FHFA Default and Prepayment Model V2, Normalized

## Table 7

**Black Knight Credit Model, Normalized**

| Capital Charges in Dollars Normalized to 100 (New Originations) | Simulation Start Year (as of September 30th) | | | | | |
|---|---|---|---|---|---|---|
| Origination Year | 2003 | 2005 | 2006 | 2007 | 2008 | 2010 |
| 2001 | | | | | | |
| 2002 | | | | | | |
| 2003 | | | | | | |
| 2004 | | | | | | |
| 2005 | | 100 | | 82 | | 68 |
| 2006 | | | | | | |
| 2007 | | | | 100 | | 92 |
| 2008 | | | | | | |
| 2009 | | | | | | |
| 2010 | | | | | | 100 |

## Table 8

**ADCO LDM Credit Model, Normalized**

| Capital Charges in Dollars Normalized to 100 (New Originations) | Simulation Start Year (as of September 30th) | | | | | |
|---|---|---|---|---|---|---|
| Origination Year | 2003 | 2005 | 2006 | 2007 | 2008 | 2010 |
| 2001 | | | | | | |
| 2002 | | | | | | |
| 2003 | | | | | | |
| 2004 | | | | | | |
| 2005 | | 100 | | 73 | | 37 |
| 2006 | | | | | | |
| 2007 | | | | 100 | | 63 |
| 2008 | | | | | | |
| 2009 | | | | | | |
| 2010 | | | | | | 100 |

For the most part, all of the models show that the dollar-denominated countercyclical capital requirement falls in each year subsequent to acquisition, consistent with the Smith and Weiher design goal of full capitalization at acquisition. One of the two exceptions observed in the Model V1 and Model V2 results is easily explained. The exception is that the absolute level of capital increases for the 2005 loans in 2006 even though the percentage requirement was lower in 2006 for both models. This occurs because Smith and Weiher chose

September 30 rather than December 31 "as of" dates for their portfolio analyses, and for the 2005 cohort in particular, a significant number of loans were not acquired by Fannie Mae until after September. These loans were not observable until the 2006 data snapshot.[6]

The other exception, again observed in Model V1 and Model V2 results, is that the absolute capital requirements increase between 2008 and 2010 for a number of origination years. For most of those origination years, the capital requirement increase between 2008 and 2010 does not result in a 2010 capital requirement that exceeds the origination year capital requirement (normalized at 100). However, for 2008 originations in Model V2 only, the absolute requirement in 2010 does modestly exceed the origination year requirement. This result suggests the Smith and Weiher design goal of full capitalization at acquisition may not always be achieved.

An in-depth investigation into the matter showed that loans 90-days or more delinquent or in the process of foreclosure climbed sharply between 2008 and 2010. Though this occurred for all origination-year cohorts, it is most noticeable in the Table 6 results for the 2008 originations. Two years later, however, a full eight percent of those loans were seriously delinquent or awaiting foreclosure. Neither Model V1 nor Model V2 predicted that so many loans would be non-performing and, at the same time, still on the books.[7] A number of factors can result in the deterioration of a loan or cohort of loans over time that may not have been predicted one, two, five, or thirty years out by the credit models. Models may be missing important explanatory variables or data availability may be such that certain borrower or loan characteristics, such as credit worthiness or loan-to-value (LTV), change over time but cannot be modeled dynamically or completely. For example, if a higher proportion of borrowers add second mortgages post-origination than has occurred historically, as may have occurred during the crisis years, then post origination LTV will increase (along with risk of default) beyond any level that could have been

---

[6] The 2005 origination-year cohort balance as of September 30, 2005 (the portfolio as-of date) was $57.4 billion. The countercyclical capital requirement (Table 1) is 9.97 percent of that amount or $5.7 billion. The balance of the 2005-origination year cohort on September 30, 2006 was $63.9 billion. It was higher because loans were originated in October, November and December of 2005 and they show up in the September 30, 2006 balance and outweigh any 2005-origination loans that ran off in the first nine months of 2006. This is not a flaw in the countercyclical conceptual framework so much as a judgment error in selecting the datasets for analysis, which could easily be rectified by choosing December 31st instead of September 30th as the portfolio "as-of" dates.

[7] We suspect that had we run the Black Knight and ADCO LDM models on the 2008 sample, it is likely that we would have found similar issues.

anticipated in the models. Additionally, the distributional characteristics of the portfolio to which the model is applied may be skewed relative to those of the historical dataset used for estimation. Lastly, structural shifts such as changes in underwriting standards, tax laws or foreclosure moratoriums may impact delinquencies and defaults in ways not anticipated by the models.

In testing, we found that when loans remained current over time, countercyclical capital requirements invariably decreased in each successive year post-origination. But, when loans became delinquent, particularly severely delinquent, yet remained on the books due to extended foreclosure timelines, countercyclical capital requirements could increase with time and to more than the level modeled at origination. Nonetheless, as occurred during the recent crisis, in those instances where the fraction of severely delinquent loans increased dramatically from year to year, the fraction of loans remaining current (and for which capital requirements fall each successive year) was almost always high enough to dominate, indicating that the countercyclical capital requirement for that cohort of loans usually, but not always, still fell each period.

As discussed above, the one exception where full capitalization at acquisition is not achieved occurs during the height of the crisis. Any firm adhering to the countercyclical capital requirements leading up to that period would have been confronted with excessive capital requirements for, and hence likely would not have acquired, many of the loans that would later fail and be responsible for this result. Additionally, the sheer number of loans in the foreclosure pipeline resulted in extended timelines and related costs that would be even more extended in the countercyclical scenario, as it was more severe than the recent credit crisis.[8] If foreclosure timelines and related costs were tied to the magnitude of house price depreciation (a future research topic), more loans would be modeled to remain in seriously delinquent and in process of foreclosure status for longer periods of time, thereby increasing the up-front capital requirement, perhaps sufficiently to ensure full capitalization at acquisition. Finally, the exception to full capitalization occurred for only one of many cohorts such that the aggregate capitalization across cohorts would have left the firm with more than sufficient capital, and importantly no need to raise additional capital post acquisition.

---

[8] Most credit models incorporate a combination of historical and projected data inputs, including but not limited to foreclosure timelines and related costs. Because our simulations used recent versions of the models, our 2005 – 2010 simulations incorporated the foreclosure timelines and related costs observed during the most recent credit crisis.

Nonetheless, this exception to the expected result of full capitalization does lead to a recommendation: cross capitalization among cohorts that is sufficient to achieve full capitalization at acquisition could be ensured if the firm (or regulator) implemented a rule governing a slower release of capital than would be dictated by rerunning the countercyclical stress test each period. For example, as observable by the results in tables 5-8, a rule that permitted a release of only 50 percent of any capital reduction dictated by the stress testing updates would provide more than a sufficient cushion to cover the 2008 cohort exception to full capitalization.

Levels: Table 9 summarizes the origination-year countercyclical capital requirements across credit models. Model V2 and Black Knight produce very similar results, and V1 and ADCO LDM also produce very similar results, but these two pairs of results differ by almost two to one. There can be many reasons for this outcome, including differences in dependent variables, included explanatory variables, and the historical data used to calibrate each model[9]. Further, these credit models are frequently updated, so any currently observed similarity or difference in results may not hold over time. It is, however, not within the scope of this paper to assess why the model results are different, just to note that they can be and to understand the consequences as they relate to the countercyclical capital requirement. We attempt to address those consequences with the back-test results below.

**Table 9**

| Model | 2005 | 2007 | 2010 |
|---|---|---|---|
| V1 | 9.97% | 16.88% | 2.62% |
| V2 | 5.64% | 9.02% | 0.69% |
| Black Knight | 6.08% | 10.49% | 0.83% |
| ADCO LDM | 9.57% | 14.46% | 1.13% |
| Mean | 7.82% | 12.71% | 1.32% |

Our results do suggest that an entity, when applying any given stress test using more than one credit model, could find substantial differences in results across models. This is largely unrelated to the specifics of the countercyclical design. These differences would likely hold true for any stress test and, as explained above, are potentially a function of several different factors related to

---

[9] Two similarly specified models can yield very different results if calibrated using different data samples. This is because the coefficients attached to the explanatory variables in each model will reflect the relationships persisting or specific to each data sample.

credit model and dataset construction. One might conclude from these results, therefore, that over-reliance on any one credit model may not be prudent or consistent with best practice.

**Historical Back-Test**

This historical back test is a means of assessing whether the countercyclical stress test is severe enough to generate capital requirements that, if met by an entity, are of a sufficient magnitude to prevent the insolvency of that entity when subjected to a severe financial stress.[10] For the severe financial stress, we focus on the recent house price cycle, which was more severe than any other previous cycle in our historical data reaching back to 1975. For the entity, we select Fannie Mae, a company that was exposed to substantial mortgage credit risk during the recent house price cycle, and which suffered substantial credit losses in connection with that exposure.

Fannie Mae's credit related losses over the recent house price cycle well exceeded their capital levels. As the crisis unfolded, the federal government placed Fannie Mae in conservatorship, essentially entering into an arrangement where the government provided Fannie Mae with capital as necessary to cover losses.

Since the beginning of 2012, Fannie Mae has not needed to draw any additional funds from the government to cover losses. Allowing that most if not all of the recent house price cycle related losses have by now been incurred by Fannie Mae, we can estimate the amount of capital Fannie Mae ultimately would have needed to have survived the cycle without government support. Specifically, this estimate will reflect capital required as of the end of 2008, soon after Fannie Mae was put into conservatorship and just before its initial draw of funds from the government.

As of September 30, 2008, Fannie Mae had $15.6 billion in its combined loss reserves (allowance for loan losses and reserve for guaranty losses) and $9.3 billion in total stockholders' equity, totaling about $24.9 billion in available capital.[11] Fannie Mae began to draw capital from the government under the

---

[10] The standard of preventing insolvency implies that there is sufficient capital for the entity to continue operations through the crisis and beyond, which would be more than our estimate of required capital. Our estimate for purposes of this back-test is limited to only that amount sufficient to cover credit losses.

[11] Federal National Mortgage Association, 10-Q report for the quarter ended September 30, 2008, Commission File No.: 0 – 50231, Balance Sheet data, p. 142.

Fannie Mae, Treasury, and FHFA Preferred Stock Purchase Agreement in early 2009 to cover a negative equity position as of December 31, 2008. Through 2011, Fannie Mae received a cumulative total of $117.1 billion (no draws were received for performance in 2012-2013). Over this same period, Fannie Mae paid $19.8 billion in dividends to the Treasury, essentially covered by their draws.[12] Thus, their draws net of dividends were $97.3 billion. Adding net draws to the beginning available capital of $24.9 billion sums to a total of $122.2 billion, which represents the minimum level of credit risk capital Fannie Mae would have needed in 2008 to have remained solvent throughout the house price cycle.[13, 14]

Before proceeding with the back-test analysis, we must first acknowledge that during the run-up to Fannie Mae being put into conservatorship, their regulator at that time, the Office of Housing Enterprise Oversight (OFHEO) lacked the authority to implement a flexible stress test, such as the countercyclical stress test proposed here. Rather, the methodology for calculating Fannie Mae's capital requirements was mandated by very specific statutory language contained in the Federal Housing Enterprises Financial Safety and Soundness Act of 1992. With hindsight, we are now aware that the biggest limitation of the 1992 Act was the requirement to base the capital charge on a stress test based on a worst-case historical experience. Unfortunately, the observable worst case experience at the time the rule was written proved to be not nearly as severe, in terms of a shock to HPI, as would occur during the 2008-2011 time period. In essence, the stress test severity imposed by the 1992 Act was required to be static, affixed to an historical level. Alternatively, the countercyclical stress test proposed by Smith and Weiher is dynamic, which adjusts the severity of the stress test to current conditions and importantly allows for levels of stress that can exceed previous historical levels. For example, assuming the countercyclical stress test was applied using the least conservative Model V2, then those requirements at the end of 2008 would have been about 4.5 percent of Fannie Mae's $3.109 trillion mortgage credit book of business, or $138.7 billion. Thus, the countercyclical credit risk capital requirements would have exceeded the $122.2 billion in forthcoming Fannie Mae losses. In other words, the required capital should have been more than sufficient

---

[12] Draw requests were $1 billion (initial liquidation preference), plus $15.2 billion (2008), $60.0 billion (2009), $15.0 billion (2010) and $25.9 billion (2011) for a total of $117.1. Dividend payments were $2.5 billion (2009), $7.7 billion (2010), $9.6 (2011), $11.6 (2012), and $72.8 billion (2013, through Q3) for a total of $105.2.

[13] At a minimum, additional capital would have been required to address market risk and operational risk capital requirements.

[14] Our calculation makes no assumptions about the payment of dividends or the rate of return on capital.

to have kept Fannie Mae from achieving negative shareholder equity with a cushion of about $16.5 billion, or 13.5 percent. This presumes that the $58.3 billion in Fannie Mae's combined loss reserves as of the end of 2011, and built up with the draw amounts, will prove to not materially over- or under-state the amount necessary to cover the house price cycle credit losses still to come post 2011.[15]

Because all of the other credit models we examined estimated even higher percentage capital requirements than Model V2, we can conclude that the Smith and Weiher stress test, as currently designed, would produce conservative capital requirements. Below in the section on the price cycle trough, we discuss how the design of the stress test leads to this result.

This back test constitutes a rigorous test of robustness for the Smith and Weiher countercyclical regime. The key parameters of their stress test were determined from data prior to the recent house price cycle. Since this recent cycle achieved an amplitude above trend (nationwide) of more than 2.5 times that observed in any previous cycle existent in the 1975-2001 historical data used by Smith and Weiher, there would be no reason to assume a priori that their countercyclical stress test would have provided for sufficient capital for a stress event outside of the historical experience. The fact that the stress test did provide for more than sufficient capital in the back test suggests that the dynamic structure of the Smith and Weiher countercyclical methodology is appropriately calibrated and likely to produce adequate, if not conservative, capital requirements going forward.

**The Countercyclical versus Actual Trough**

Perhaps the most important yet least developed component of the Smith and Weiher methodology is the criteria for defining the trough of the HPI shock. Establishing a pre-set trough is key to defining the severity of the HPI shock component of the countercyclical stress test. They establish a trough (at the state level) by identifying the lowest level that real HPI has fallen below trend (expressed in real terms as a percentage of trend) based on historical data from 1975-2001. Smith and Weiher did have the advantage of observing the first few years of the recent house price cycle and state that their methodology was sufficiently successful in that it did happen to establish troughs that were lower

---

[15] Federal National Mortgage Association, 10-K report for the fiscal year ended December 31, 2011, Commission File No.: 0 – 50231, Table 12, p. 101.

than realized troughs in the recent severe cycle for all but about five states. More complete and recent data reveal that the troughs Smith and Weiher projected were in fact sufficient for all but eleven states, and they understated the extent of the trough for four of those states by less than five percent.

Figure 1 offers an updated comparison of the level of the countercyclical predicted troughs identified using 1975-2001 data with the respective troughs actually observed in each state between January, 2008 and April, 2013. During the last housing crisis, actual troughs were within plus or minus five percent of the countercyclical predicted troughs for 30.4 percent of the national housing stock. Actual troughs were more than five percent above the countercyclical predicted troughs for about 53 percent of housing stock, meaning the stress test would have over-predicted capital for that portion of the market. Actual troughs were below the countercyclical predicted troughs for about 38 percent of the housing market, but for the majority of these states, the extent of under prediction was minor. Actual troughs were more than five percent below the predicted troughs for only about 16 percent of the housing stock. As evidenced by the back-test presented above, and assuming a geographically diversified portfolio, we can conclude from these magnitudes that the understatement of capital for the few states where the actual trough was deeper than that projected by the countercyclical methodology would likely be more than compensated for by the overstatement of capital for the many states where actual troughs were shallower than the countercyclical stress trough.

In general, we find that because all states were not equally impacted in the recent house price crisis, by imposing a severe shock on all states simultaneously, the countercyclical methodology will likely be biased to overstate rather than understate any resulting capital requirement (or at least provide for sufficient capital should a future house price cycle affect all states equally). As new cycles are completed, the Smith and Weiher trend and trough levels should be updated, such that for those states where the actual troughs exceeded the countercyclical predicted troughs, new countercyclical predicted troughs will be generated that would correct for any prior trough prediction error.

## Figure 1
## Since January 2008, the Lowest Level of Real HPI
## Relative to the Trough
## (Projected with 1975-2001 Data)

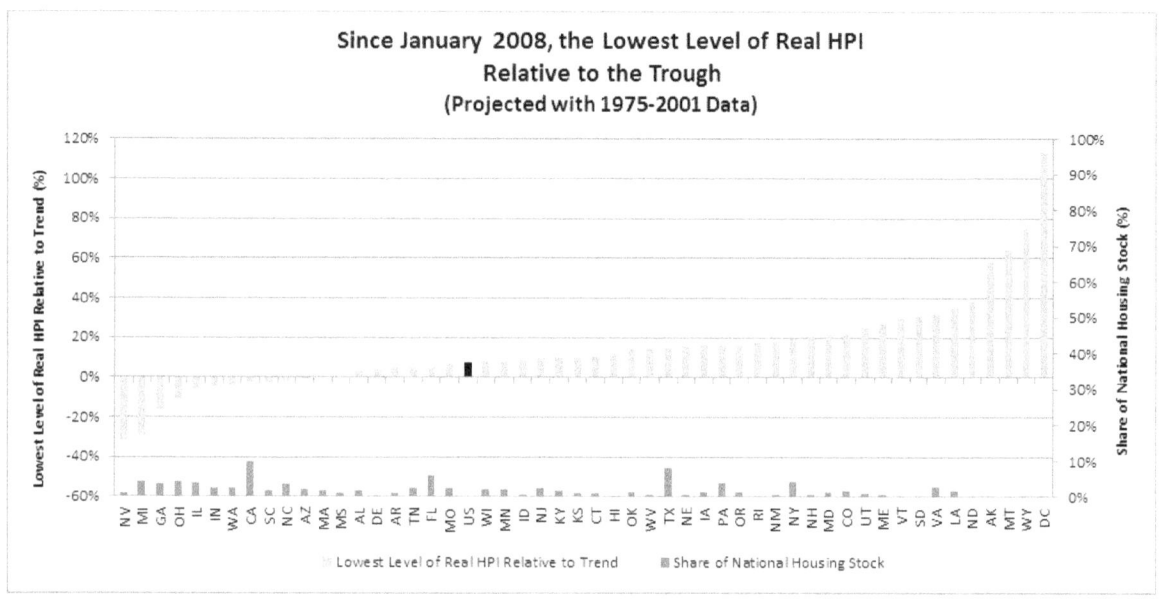

The success of the countercyclical trough methodology when applied to the recent severe HPI cycle may at first seem surprising given that the methodology was based on data only through 2001.  But the fact that historical troughs (defined in terms of percentage below trend) were not breached for over 80 percent of states suggests that there may be an underlying economic rationale that is largely consistent with the Smith and Weiher method.  For example, as housing prices are falling, there is likely some level at which many investors perceive that prices are sufficiently below trend to assure a reasonable return on investing in housing assets, thus invigorating demand sufficiently to stall any further house price decline.   Such a level, if based purely on rate of return, would be consistent across cycles.

A review of the data on the recent house price cycle, as shown in Figure 2, demonstrates that there is asymmetry in the cycle about the trend, such that the proportion that house prices may rise above trend does not correlate with how far prices will subsequently fall below trend.  This can happen if, for example, the time prices stay below trend is longer than they stay above trend (see also — Leamer, 2007; Case and Shiller, 2003).

21

## Figure 2
## Maximums Above and Minimums below Trend
## By State since January, 2006

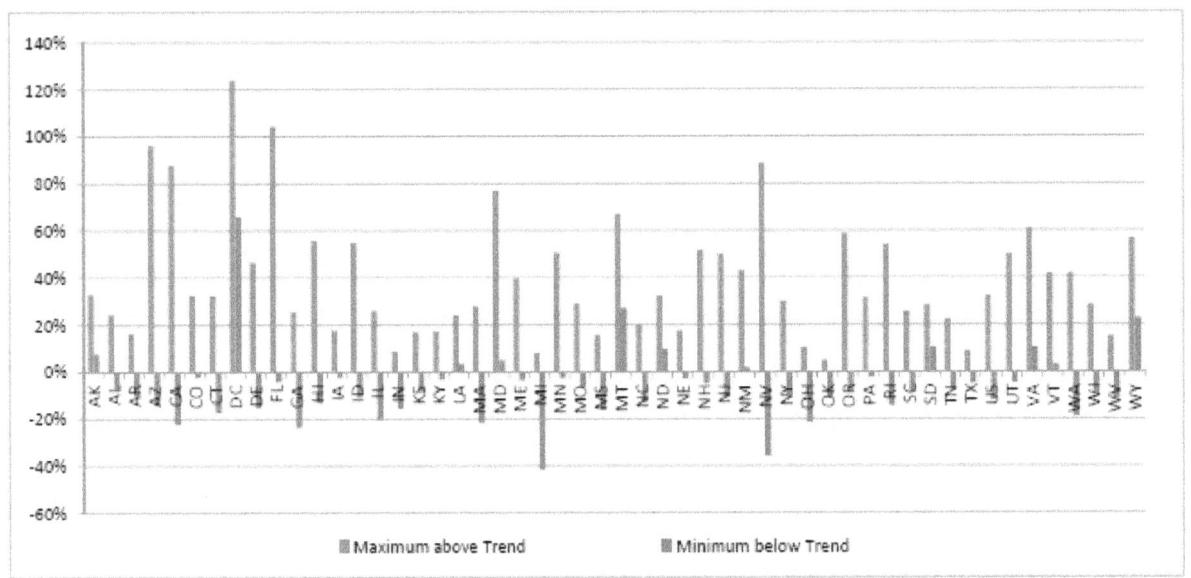

Data on how far below trend HPI has fallen over several cycles is presented in Figure 3. It is noteworthy that even though the recent cycle constituted a rise in HPI above trend that was more than double that seen in the earlier major cycles, it did not result in HPI falling below trend by a farther amount than in previous cycles. These data appear to support the idea that there is a depth for the trough relative to trend that persists across cycles with different upside amplitudes, and that depth is generally no more than 20-25 percent below trend.

**Figure 3**
**Distribution of State-Level Troughs**
**1975-Present**

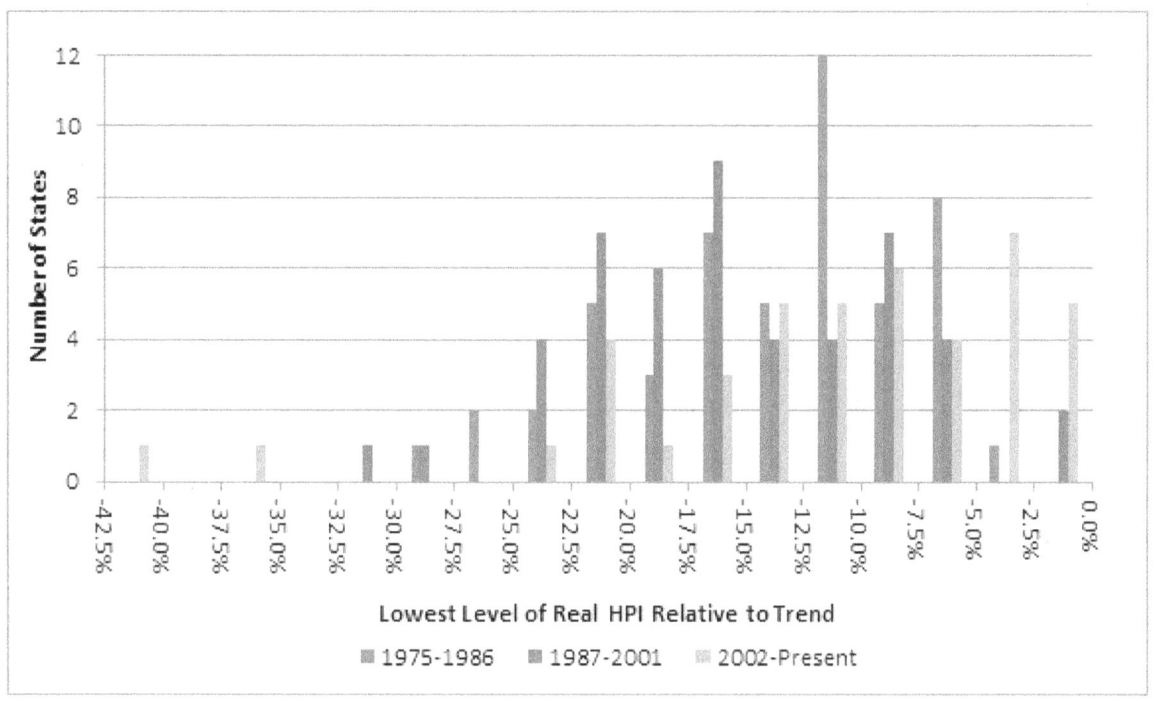

**Robustness of HPI Trend**

The trend line is an important element of the countercyclical methodology because it is tied to the determination of the trough, and ultimately the HPI recovery path, both of which affect the severity of the test. Smith and Weiher did not attempt to extend the time series used to determine the HPI trend beyond the end of 2001 and into the current house price cycle because, at the time of their analysis, it was clear for many states that HPI was still at or near a cycle trough, meaning that the house price cycle that started in the 2002-3 time period was not yet complete. Including an incomplete cycle in the data being used to generate the trend line would only result in a biased trend line.

As of April, 2013, our cutoff for this analysis, the most recent house price cycle was arguably not complete, given that real HPI for the U.S. (weighted average of states), although rising, was still 2.6 percent below the pre-2002 trend line level. Nonetheless, we considered the cycle near enough to completion to at least investigate how regeneration of the trend line using data from January 1975 through April 2013 might adjust the state-level trend lines, which are used to generate the countercyclical HPI shocks.

Updating the trend line only has consequences for the countercyclical stress test if it is materially different from the prior trend. In order to see whether that might be the case, we examined the old and new trend lines for all 50 states. We present evidence for three states which, combined, are remarkably representative of 48 states, accounting for 99.4 percent of the housing stock.[16] The three states are California, characteristic of 12 mostly western states; Kansas, characteristic of 20 mostly southern and mid-western states; and New York, characteristic of 16 mostly east coast states.

Figure 4 shows for California the real HPI, the old and new trend lines, and the HPI troughs and time path for the countercyclical stress test that corresponds to each trend line. The new trend line appears steeper than the old, but real HPI has not yet returned to even the old trend line suggesting the current cycle is incomplete. In the coming months or year, as new observations on real HPI are incorporated, the new trend line will begin to flatten to become more closely aligned with the prior trend line. Hence, including the new cycle in the trend line calculation would have little or no consequence. This is already evident in the fact that we can observe the stress path trough will scarcely change by updating the trend line, even though the HPI shock would be based on a new actual trough.

---

[16]North and South Dakota, and the District of Columbia, are three regions for which there may have recently been a material shift in long term trend of real HPI. Given their small size and unique situations in recent years, there is an argument that the analysts' judgment may be more appropriate in setting a trend line for these regions than reliance on the Smith and Weiher one size fits all rule.

**Figure 4**
**California Real HPI, Trend and Trough Lines**
**(Based on Real HPI through 2001 versus through April, 2013)**

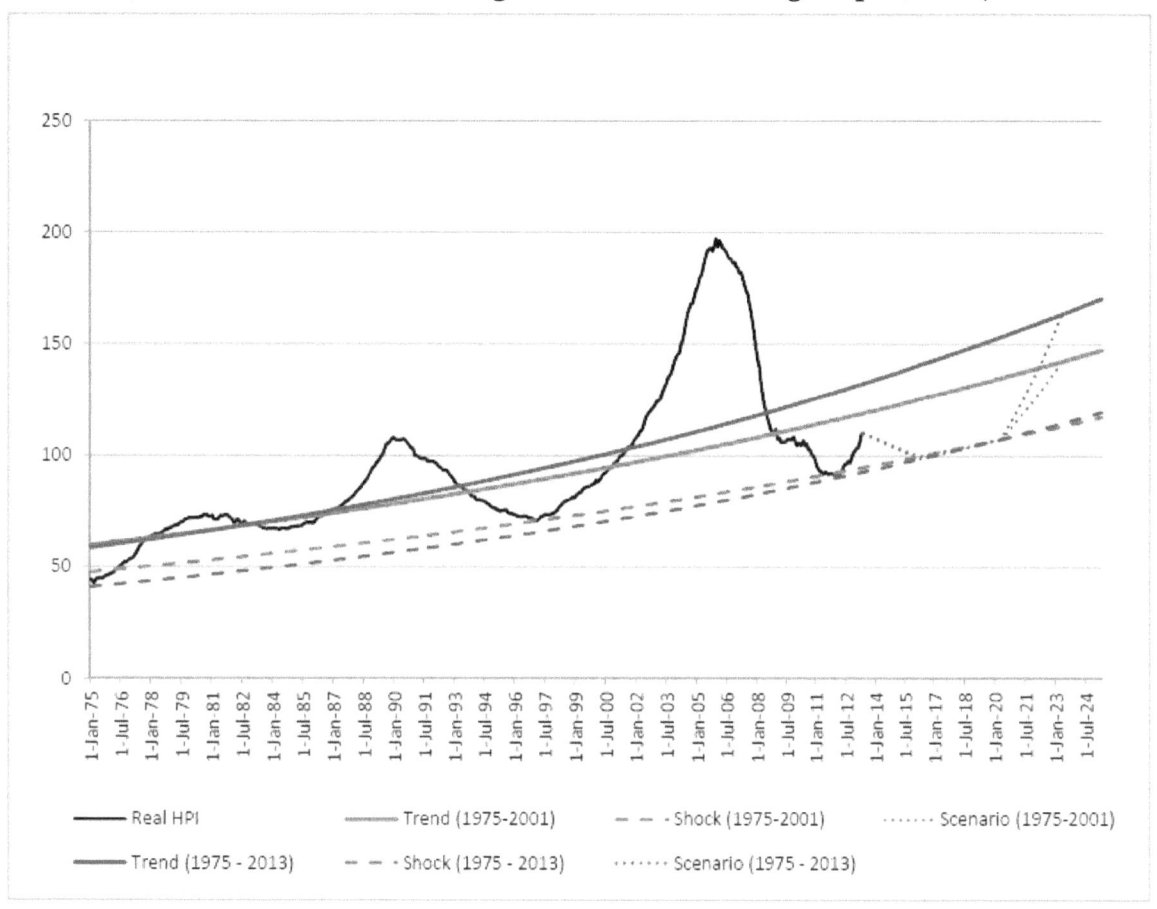

Figure 5 shows the same information for New York. It is evident that real HPI has yet to begin returning to trend. Again, as new observations are added, the new trend line will flatten to more closely resemble the old. Also, even after updating the trend line, the countercyclical trough for New York would still be based on a prior (pre-2002) experience and therefore would not be updated. Note that if the updated trend line were to be more upward sloping than the old trend line, then the severity of the countercyclical stress test (depth to which HPI would fall) would be reduced. This is because the trough is expressed as a percentage of the (higher when updated) trend line.

**Figure 5**
**New York Real HPI, Trend and Trough Lines**
**(Based on Real HPI through 2001 versus through April, 2013)**

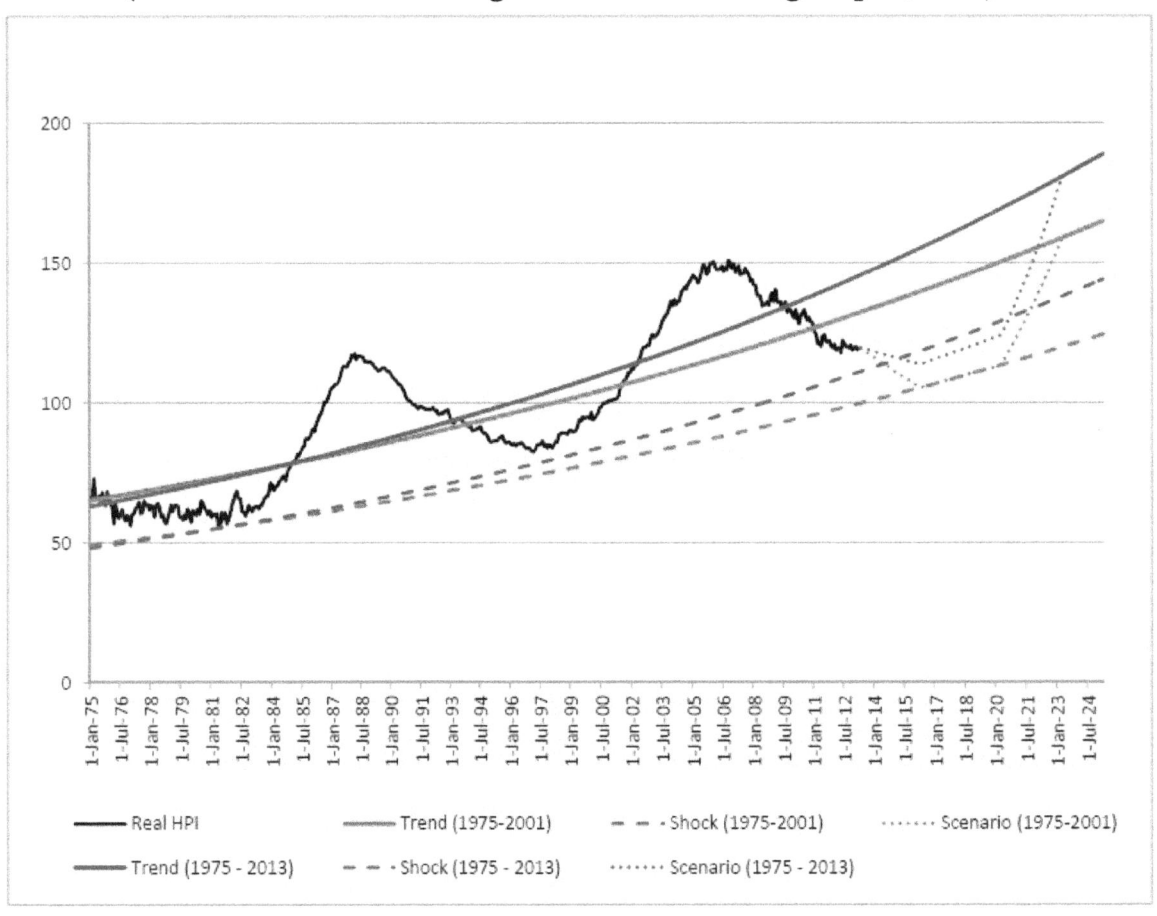

Figure 6 shows the same data for Kansas, a state with a flat trend line. Kansas and 19 other states did not experience significant house price appreciation, or at least showed more symmetry in house prices over time such that both the updated and old trend lines are flat and extremely similar. Adding the most recent house price cycle would likely have no noticeable effect on the resulting trough or trend line.

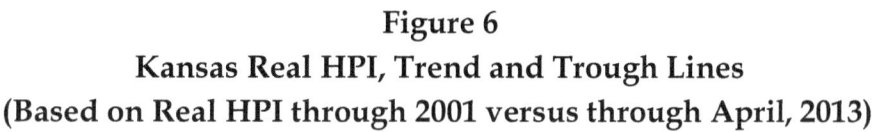

**Figure 6**
**Kansas Real HPI, Trend and Trough Lines**
**(Based on Real HPI through 2001 versus through April, 2013)**

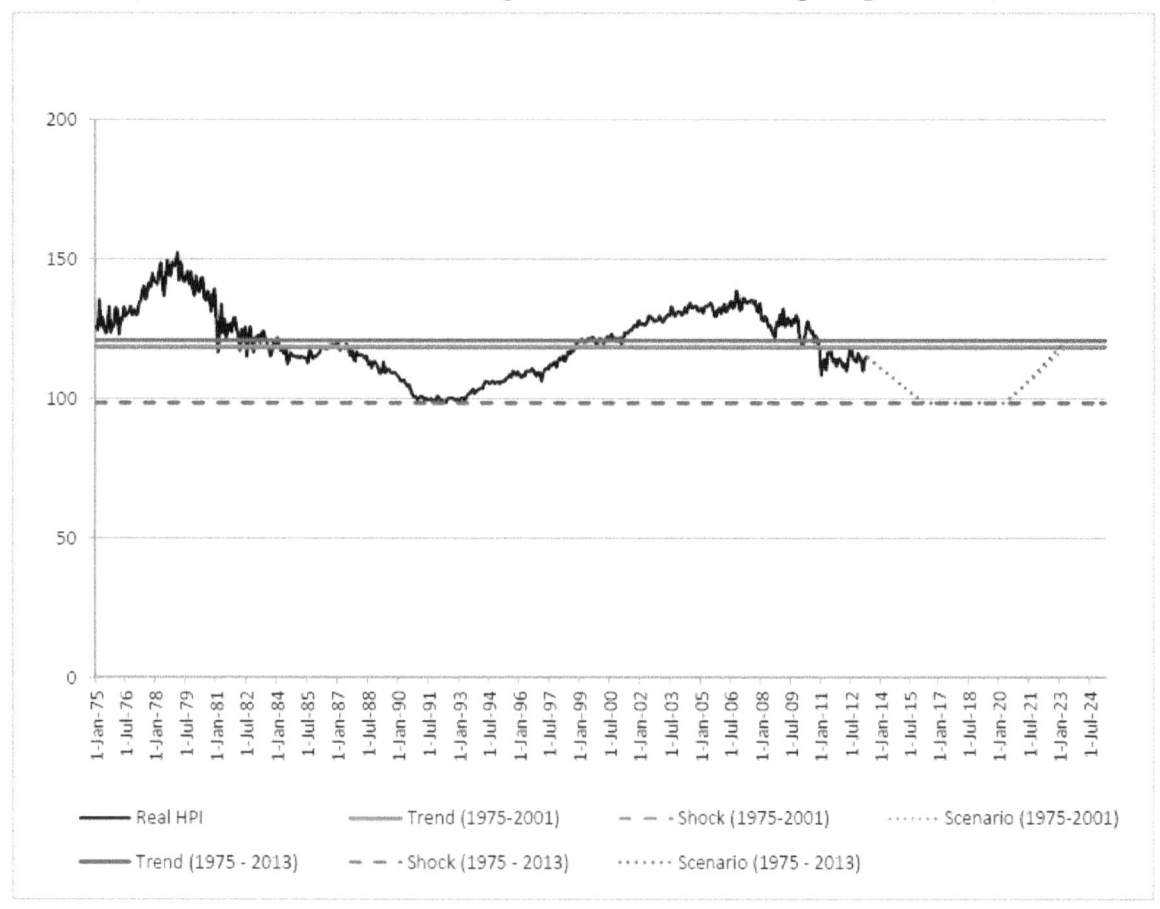

In general, this analysis suggests that updating the trend line to incorporate the most recent house price cycle would not have a material effect on the results of the countercyclical stress test. This implies that the Smith and Weiher methodological design would likely prove relatively stable over time. Such stability lends assurance that capital requirements for a pool of loans established on the day of acquisition would not be increased at a later date because of an update to the data sets used to determine the trend line and corresponding trough.

## Time Path of the Countercyclical HPI Shocks

Based upon their observations of historical state-level real HPI cycles that occurred between 1975-2001, Smith and Weiher selected a time path for their countercyclical HPI shock of three years for HPI to reach the trough, four years at trough and three years back to trend (3-4-3), for a 10 year total HPI stress path. Here we revisit the 3-4-3 assumption in light of the most recent house price cycle to determine whether the previously observed time pattern continued to persist, and if not, the materiality of any change. An important caveat, only seven years have elapsed since national real HPI peaked in 2006, which makes any comparison to the previously observed 3-4-3 pattern somewhat incomplete.

We find that, for the most part, the pattern was not representative of the recent cycle. The majority of states, particularly states with the largest populations, showed house prices falling for more than three years, with the most frequently observed house price declines of four or five years to trough. Likewise, most states did not show house prices remaining at the trough level for four years. Instead house prices began to revert to trend after only one or two years. The pattern for the U.S. as a whole (weighted average of all states) was four years to trough, two years at trough and a projected one or two years back to trend (as of April, 2013, house prices had not reverted to trend nationally).

Table 10 shows that, for all 50 states and the District of Columbia, the most frequently observed number of years from peak-to-trough in the most recent credit crisis was four years (30 states), followed by five years (13 states). Only four states showed three years of peak-to-trough HPI decline.

### Table 10

| Frequency Distribution of Years to Trough since Most Recent Peak | |
|---|---|
| **Years Peak-to-Trough** | **Frequency** |
| 1 | 2 |
| 2 | 1 |
| 3 | 4 |
| 4 | 30 |
| 5 | 13 |
| 6 | 1 |
| **Total** | **51** |

Table 11 shows that the results for the most populous states mirror those of all states in general with four being the most frequently observed number of years from peak-to-trough. Two and three years at trough are observed nearly equally and the majority of states have not yet seen house prices return to trend.

### Table 11
#### Real HPI Decline and Time at Trough (most populous states)

| State | Population | HPI Decline (Peak to Trough) | Time at Trough (If applicable) |
|---|---|---|---|
| California | 37,253,956 | 3 | 3 |
| Texas | 25,145,561 | 4 | 1 |
| New York | 19,378,102 | 5 | 2 |
| Florida | 18,801,310 | 3 | 3 |
| Illinois | 12,830,632 | 4 | 2 |
| Pennsylvania | 12,702,379 | 5 | 1 |
| Ohio | 11,536,504 | 5 | 2 |
| Michigan | 9,883,640 | 4 | 3 |
| Georgia | 9,687,653 | 4 | 1 |
| North Carolina | 9,535,483 | 4 | 2 |
| New Jersey | 8,791,894 | 4 | 2 |
| Virginia | 8,001,024 | 2 | 3 |
| **Weighted Average** | | **4** | **2** |

Note: HPI Recovery (trough to trend) is not shown because most states had either not reached their troughs by April, 2013 or, if they had, real HPI had not yet returned to trend.

Given the patterns observed in the most recent credit crisis, we generated four alternative countercyclical house price paths:

- Four years to trough, two at trough and two back to trend (4-2-2),
- Four years to trough, three at trough and two back to trend (4-3-2),
- Four years to trough, three at trough and three back to trend (4-3-3), and
- Four years to trough, four at trough and three back to trend (4-4-3).

Figure 7 shows the baseline (3-4-3) and alternative house price shock paths for New York (NY) as of Q3, 2007. The real HPI shocks are identical as a percent of trend (24.49 percent below trend), but because NY has an upward-sloping trend line, the length of time for the initial leg of the stress path affects the ultimate depth of the shock. Specifically, applying the 3-4-3 path, we reach the trough of 24.49

percent below the trend 36 months out where the value of HPI at trend is 125.27 resulting in a trough level of 94.59. Applying the 4-2-2 path, we reach the trough of 24.49 percent below the trend 48 months out where the value of HPI at trend is 127.58, resulting in a trough level of 96.34. This means that for states with upward-sloping trend lines, applying a time path where the trough is reached sooner will result in a lower trough and more stressful test. For states with flat trend lines, a shorter first leg will result in a trough that is reached sooner, but will not be lower than troughs from alternative paths. In either case, countercyclical losses should be higher, everything else equal, the shorter the first leg.

### Figure 7
### New York Real HPI, Trend Line, Trough Line
### Baseline and Alternative HPI Shock Paths

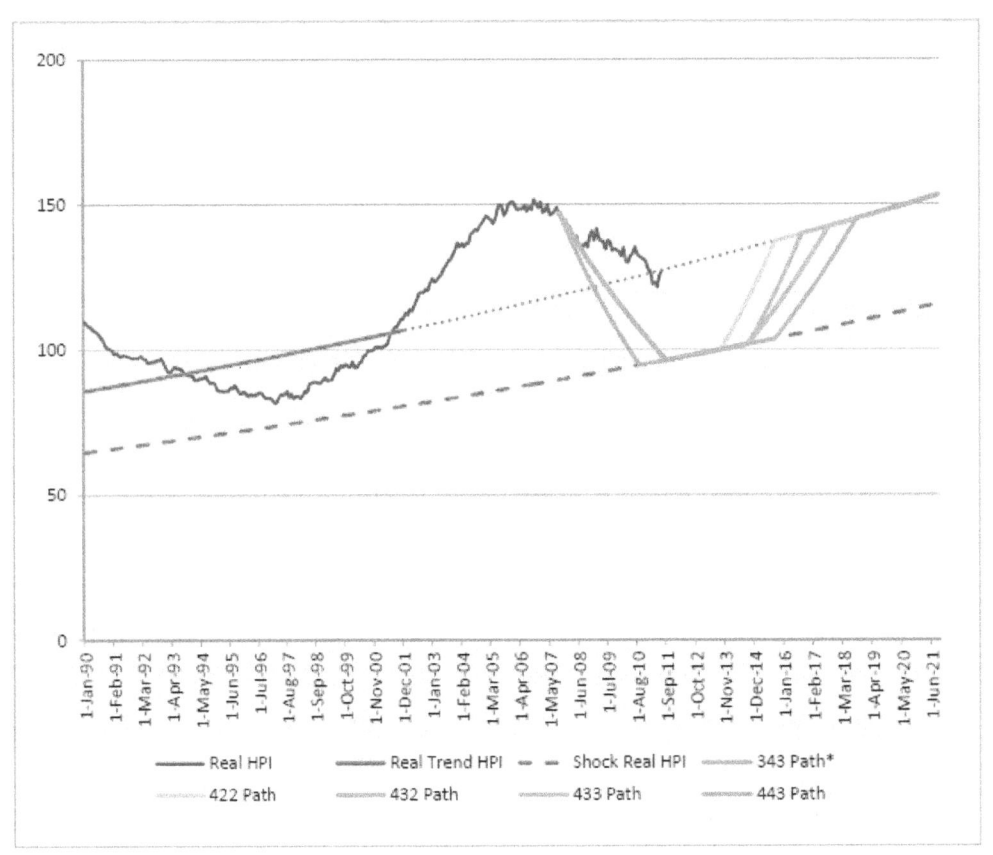

Additionally, on a discounted present value basis, losses that occur earlier would be expected to contribute more to total losses than those that occur later. So, we expect that the length of the first leg (or time to trough) should matter most, the length of the second leg (or time at trough) should matter second-most and the length of the third leg (or time back to trend) should matter least in terms of countercyclical losses.

We tested each of the alternative paths vis-à-vis the baseline (3-4-3) path to identify the impact on estimated losses using the Black Knight and ADCO LDM credit models. We used the same two million sample of loans as in prior analyses but focused on those loans outstanding only as of Q3, 2007 for the comparative length and timing of the alternative countercyclical house price shocks.[17]

Table 12 shows the results for the ADCO LDM credit model. Results for the Black Knight model were similar. Overall countercyclical losses are nearly 150 basis points lower due to the extension of the time to trough by one year (and it being marginally higher as well) along with the shortening of the second and third legs by one year. Of the four alternative time paths, the one with the lowest losses (4-2-2) also is the shortest in total length back to trend, eight years. The extension of the second leg from two to three years (4-2-2 to 4-3-2) increases losses overall by about 20 basis points. Incrementally, the extension of the third leg by one year from two to three years (4-3-2 to 4-3-3) increases losses by an additional four basis points. Then, extending the middle leg again from three years to four years (4-3-3 to 4-4-3) increases losses by an additional 12 basis points.

### Table 12
#### ADCO LDM Credit Model

| Capital Charges as Percent of UPB (UPB at start of simulation) | 2007 Start Year (as of September 30th) | | | | |
|---|---|---|---|---|---|
| Origination Year | 3-4-3 | 4-2-2 | 4-3-2 | 4-3-3 | 4-4-3 |
| 2001 | 1.71% | 1.49% | 1.53% | 1.54% | 1.56% |
| 2002 | 1.95% | 1.61% | 1.64% | 1.65% | 1.68% |
| 2003 | 1.57% | 1.20% | 1.23% | 1.24% | 1.26% |
| 2004 | 3.92% | 2.98% | 3.07% | 3.09% | 3.14% |
| 2005 | 8.05% | 6.49% | 6.67% | 6.72% | 6.83% |
| 2006 | 13.26% | 11.11% | 11.40% | 11.47% | 11.66% |
| 2007 | 14.46% | 12.21% | 12.56% | 12.65% | 12.88% |
| Total | 8.02% | 6.64% | 6.83% | 6.87% | 6.99% |

The Smith and Weiher assumption that house prices would fall simultaneously in all states following the most frequently-observed time path of

---

[17] Of the three samples used throughout this study (Q3, 2005, Q3, 2007 and Q3, 2010), the Q3, 2007 sample was selected for the time path analysis because it was closest to the peak of the house price cycle for most states.

three years to trough, four years at trough and three years back to trend based on data through 2001 did not materialize in the most recent crisis. Instead, four alternative time paths were observed. Results generated using the four alternative time paths followed expectations, and showed that the longer house prices stay suppressed the higher are stress losses. But, losses are not materially higher if the extension of time at trough or time back to trend is extended only by one year. The Smith and Weiher assumption of a 3-4-3 house price time path, then, is not unreasonable and if anything proved conservative as applied to the recent house price cycle.

## Conclusions and Future Research

The tests of robustness presented herein support the conclusion that the Smith and Weiher countercyclical capital regime should produce capital requirements sufficient to ensure an entity would remain solvent during severe house price cycles. This conclusion is strongly supported by the positive result of the back-test, where the resulting capital requirement proved conservative even though the key components of the stress test were based on pre-2002 data. Individual examinations of the trend line, trough, and time path components all indicate that the underlying methodology is stable and robust. We also find that the countercyclical-related patterns in capital requirements will not vary when the stress test is applied to different credit models, but the level of capital required may vary appreciably. This suggests that over-reliance on any one credit model may not be prudent.

Based on our analyses, we find three areas for future research. The first is to develop a theoretical basis for determining the HPI trough used in the stress test. Such a model would incorporate the micro-financial incentives driving buyers' and investors' decisions to re-enter a declining house price market, while perhaps also incorporating other macro determinants affecting the speed and depth of house price declines.

The second area concerns the degree of aggregation involved in the application of the countercyclical framework to credit models. This issue is not unique to countercyclical stress testing, and occurs on two fronts. The first to be examined is the potential for any bias in the estimated capital requirements that might follow from the degree or manner in which loans are aggregated or bucketed to reduce computation time. For example, we expect that a coarse bucketing of particularly important explanatory variables will lead to lower estimated credit losses as the tails of the loss distribution where losses are amplified are likely to be muted or lost in the process of aggregation. The second aggregation issue to be examined concerns the geographic or regional level at which the countercyclical stress test is applied. Smith and Weiher only examine their test applied at the state level. The data exists to apply the countercyclical stress test at the MSA or even more local level. We would anticipate that the non-linearity of credit losses with respect to HPI, combined with more volatile HPI cycles at local levels, would mean that the countercyclical capital requirements should be higher the more granular, or geographically disaggregated the stress path. The question is by how much, and what is the tradeoff in accuracy.

The third area is to develop a methodology to adjust assumptions or models of foreclosure timelines and related costs to correspond with the severity of the countercyclical stress test. The extension of foreclosure timelines during periods of extreme stress via moratoriums or overwhelmed judicial systems has proven to be a significant factor affecting credit losses. Because the countercyclical capital regime involves a dynamically changing level of stress, the foreclosure timelines should likewise be gauged to the level of stress.

# References

Case, Karl E. and Robert J. Shiller, "Is There a Bubble in the Housing Market?," *Brookings Papers on Economic Activity*, vol. 34(2), 2003.

Cordell, Larry, Liang Geng, Laurie Goodman and Lidan Yang, "The Cost of Delay," *Federal Reserve Bank of Atlanta*, Working Paper No. 13-15, April, 2013.

Dunsky, Robert M. and Thomas S.Y. Ho, "Valuing Fixed Rate Mortgage Loans with Default and Prepayment Options," *The Journal of Fixed Income*, 16(4), Spring, 2007.

Frame, Scott W., Kristopher Gerardi and Paul S. Willen, "The Failure of Supervisory Stress Testing: OFHEO's Risk-Based Capital Model for Fannie Mae and Freddie Mac," *Federal Reserve Bank of Atlanta*, Working Paper, December, 2013.

Leamer, Edward E., "Housing is the Business Cycle," *Proceedings, Federal Reserve Bank of Kansas City*, September, 2007.

Smith, Scott and Jesse Weiher, "Countercyclical Capital Regime: A Proposed Design and Empirical Evaluation," *Federal Housing Finance Agency*, Working Paper No. 12-2, April, 2012.